PRECIOUS
were the
HOURS

POEMS AND OTHER RUMINATIONS
FROM AN OLD BABY BOOMER

JOHN LARRABEE

ISBN: 978-0-578-73498-9

Published by Hummingbird Press
Swanville, Maine, USA

Cover Photo by Rebecca Tripp

Cover Design and Interior Layout by Tami Boyce

A NOTE FROM THE AUTHOR

Dear Reader:

Poetry is not for everyone. I never really enjoyed it much until a few years ago. I guess it's like many things in our busy lives that we take for granted, until one day we suddenly realize that time is running out. That's when we begin to look at life through a different lens.

Instead of being lost in the hectic day-to-day events of building a career and raising a family we find ourselves in a more relaxed and reflective mood. If we are so fortunate as to have grandchildren, we cherish even more our close family ties.

We try to reconnect with high school friends as old memories begin to resurface. Sometimes unsettling current events leave us longing for earlier and simpler times. We think more about the aura of the natural world we will leave behind as the vibrancy of our own world slowly recedes.

Aging is not unlike the seasonal changes that take place in the northern and southern hemispheres, and the "winter season" is a perfect analogy for this state of reflective bliss that I have been so fortunate to experience.

Those are but a few of the emotional reflections that led me to explore reading poetry for enjoyment and writing in verse as a method of self-expression.

Even if you are not a big fan of poetry, I hope you find something on these pages that will lift your spirits, put a smile on your face, or perhaps even ignite a spark that leads to your own efforts to explore the emotional range of self-expression through poetry.

Thank you for your purchase. I hope you will enjoy reading these poems as much as I have enjoyed writing them. If you would like to offer comments, suggestions, or stay up to date on our fundraising efforts, please contact me at: preciouswerethehours@gmail.com.

With warm wishes,

John Larrabee

John Larrabee
September 2020

For Angela (my "Angel")
and
Travis (my "Mentor")

Thank you for your unconditional love, for your abiding devotion,
and for giving my life meaning. I have learned more about life
and about myself from you than you will ever know.

Your selfless dedication and steadfast commitment to family
and in the service to others continues to make us
all proud and the world a better place.

v

PRAISE FOR *PRECIOUS WERE THE HOURS...*

In an unapologetic attempt to generate interest and boost sales, I reached out to a few random people, ghosts and grand poohbahs for pre-publication reviews of *Precious Were The Hours*. The responses were sparse but to the point:

"Who are you and what do you want from me?"
— A distant relative.

"Have no fear of perfection – you'll never reach it."
— Salvador Dali

"The fool doth think he is wise, but the wise man knows himself to be a fool."
— Shakespeare (Not quite sure how to take that one!)

"Seriously? A favorable review after the way your crappy poems objectify animals? GARBAGE...PURE GARBAGE!!!"
— PETA

"If your brains were dynamite, there wouldn't be enough to blow your hat off."
— Kurt Vonnegut, Jr.

"Better to remain silent and be thought a fool than to speak and to remove all doubt."
— Anonymous (I think someone stole that line from Abraham Lincoln.)

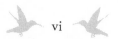

"Your mother should have dropped you and kept the stork!"
— Anonymous (Probably one of my siblings!)

"!@#$%^&*()__)(*&^%$#@Fake News!"
— DJT

But my three, 4-legged grand-dogs think I'm awesome…and gave me heartfelt reviews!

"Poetry comes fine spun from a mind at peace."

– Ovid

TABLE OF CONTENTS

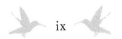

PREFACE AND INTRODUCTION

PREFACE

Do you know the difference between a book's Preface and its Introduction? Me either – which is why I combined them.

I would have included a Foreword, too, but I know that is usually a puff piece written by someone other than the author, so it would be a little awkward for me to write that. Complicating matters is the likelihood that I would have to pay someone to write nice things about me and my book!

I would rather you, the reader, decide if the book has any merit – so feel free to submit your comments. You, after all, have paid for the privilege.

So, instead of asking someone to write a Foreword I am going to include an Afterword. As the name implies, it will appear at the end of the book.

I know, it seems odd to have an Afterword if there is no Foreword, but it's my book and my rules! It's a philosophy I learned from reading Winston Churchill, who said the following when writing about his role in world affairs: *"History will be kind to me for I intend to write it."* (And he was right!)

Like the Foreword, an Afterword is usually written by someone other than the author. However, in this case I decided to write it myself. I think you will understand why when you read it.

(Remember, books are to be read from front to back, so no cheating by jumping ahead to the Afterword before you've read the book!)

INTRODUCTION

My favorite hobbies are reading nonfiction and writing letters to my children and grandchildren.

For me, reading is like stepping into a time capsule that takes me as far back in time as I wish to go, and to places where I can experience events by figuratively standing next to the men and women who helped shape the world we live in today. No book is off limits as long as it is informative and well written.

In a sense, exchanging letters with my children and grandchildren will serve a similar purpose if preserved and perpetuated over time. Letters can provide a priceless sense of personal family history and intergenerational connectedness for future generations.

Over the past couple of years I have expanded my writing to include poetry – not always the formal type that would pass muster with critics, or the creative method of free verse employed by real poets – just plain, simple poems expressing mostly real life experiences in verse rather than prose.

C. S. Lewis wrote, *"We ought not write about our actions but about our thoughts. We busy ourselves talking about the weather and the little trivial happenings of each day, while the thoughts of our hearts, the really great experiences of ourselves, are seldom mentioned."*

Without being consciously aware of it, letter writing has always given me the pleasure of expressing 'the thoughts of our hearts,' as Lewis would say, and has been one of the main reasons I have enjoyed writing for so long.

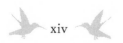

Expressing one's emotions in print can be challenging at times because the physical communications of facial expression and tone of voice are absent, but forming the writer's thoughts into carefully crafted words and phrases is part of the joy of writing – at least for me.

Writing poetry is similar in many ways. The single major difference between letter writing and writing poetry is, of course, that a writer of poetry enjoys a "poetic license" to be creative and is under no burden to speak truthfully or factually. Like a novelist, the poet can just make stuff up!

While many poems often have some basis in reality and reflect the personal experiences of the writer, there are also elements of abstract thinking and imagination that represent the essential tools for creating an emotional experience between the writer and the reader.

The challenge for the writer is to find the right balance between real life experiences and the freedom of thought that fuels his/her imaginative expression. The challenge for the reader (at least of these pages) is to stay awake – and hopefully not ask for a refund!

When first considering the idea of publishing this book, I had no concept of the immense time involved. After all, the poems were already written so I thought I could just perform a final spell check, throw on a cover and be done with it. I quickly discovered it's not quite that easy.

For starters I did my own editing, which was a HUGE mistake! I simply cannot leave anything I have written alone, so I ended up tweaking nearly every poem that appears on the following pages – some several times.

Then I had to hire a book cover designer to design an eye-catching cover and rearrange the interior layout so it wouldn't look like a jumbled mess. And, on top of that, Amazon has very strict self-publishing guidelines, so I was very fortunate to find a cover designer/interior layout specialist/Amazon guru to fill all three roles.

I must give a very special and heartfelt "Thank You" to Tami Boyce, for handling all three of those critical elements and so ably guiding me through this self-publishing process. I hope you will visit Tami's website at www.tami-boyce.com to see some of her clever work as an illustrator and book designer.

But the worst part, by far, was the terrifying idea that some of my innermost thoughts and writings would be shared with the public, and that by doing so I might embarrass my family. And, of course, there is the fear of failure – or that some poems will be misinterpreted in some way.

I have shared very few of these poems with my children and grandchildren, so I have no idea how they might react to seeing them for the first time and in a public forum. I had intended to leave them handwritten in a notebook to be discovered after my death, but, as you will learn if you make it to the end, very compelling circumstances became the deciding factor to self-publish them now.

So, as you walk with me on this incredible and humbling journey of self-expression, I hope you will keep in mind the final two lines of *The Cloths of Heaven*, by W. B. Yeats:

> *"I have spread my dreams under your feet;*
> *Tread softly because you tread on my dreams."*

Hopefully you uncover a few poems that will strike you as worthy, have an emotional impact, provoke additional thought or discovery, or even elicit a smile (or maybe a smirk). I know just how precious time is, so thank you for investing some of yours in reading *Precious Were The Hours*.

— JL

DISCLAIMER

To the best of my knowledge all of the material herein is original to me, except on the rare occasions that I borrowed a line or two, or have written a poem that closely resembles the theme or essence of another author. I have acknowledged each of those instances where they occurred.

I also read a lot – and I will often find a new or unusual word or phrase that sticks with me without remembering the source. "Tarn" (a small mountain lake) is a perfect example. The poem *Appalachia* was written around that single word, which was new to me at the time, but I am at a loss as to where I first saw it in print.

Of course there is no need to give attribution for a single word or for simple phrases, but I am very sensitive of the need to give credit where credit is due. If I have failed to attribute any substantive material it was inadvertent and not intentional. Humans have been writing for thousands of years, so it isn't always easy to write something completely original.

— JL

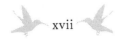

THE CLOTHS OF HEAVEN

By: William Butler Yeats

Had I the heavens' embroidered cloths,
Enwrought with golden and silver light,
The blue and the dim and the dark cloths
Of night and light and the half-light,
I would spread the cloths under your feet:
But I, being poor, have only my dreams;
I have spread my dreams under your feet;
Tread softly because you tread on my dreams.

Grandchildren are a Priceless Treasure...

NOTE: *This poem was personalized for each of my five grandchildren for their 2019 birthdays. The first line begins: "You, [Grandchild's First Name], are a priceless treasure." The remainder was unchanged.*

A GRANDPARENT'S MESSAGE

Grandchildren are a priceless treasure,
Creating such joy and endless pleasure;
The past belongs to me that's true,
But now I see the future in you.

It's in your eyes that I see...
Images of ancestors throughout history;
From ancient times and faraway places,
Hope for you is etched on their faces.

It's in your eyes that I see...
A child of God with boundless energy;
The future belongs to you, my Sweet,
And the whole world lies at your feet.

It's in your eyes that I see...
Renewed hope and opportunity;
A bold new world is taking shape,
Open to all and for each to partake.

It's in your eyes that I see...
All of God's children living in harmony;
A future that promises a better life,
Without want, hunger, fear or strife.

It's in your eyes that I see...
Images of ancestors proud as can be;
From ancient times and faraway places,
Hopes fulfilled and smiles on their faces.

PRECIOUS WERE THE HOURS

Sitting here at my writing table,
Looking out over the back yard;
Bending words with an anvil,
To fit the language of a bard.

The songbirds are on the wing,
And flitter here and there;
While in the wind chimes sing,
As life carries on everywhere.

With each blink my eyes take,
Time silently moves forward;
Leaving memories in its wake,
As the world sallies onward.

I've lived a life beyond its prime,
And caught the scent of flowers;
Oh how swiftly passed the time,
Oh so precious were the hours!

MY SHINING LIGHT

Good morning, good morning, life begins anew,
A day of hopes and dreams made just for you!
Somewhere an early sun peeks o'er distant hills,
Before shining down on fields of golden daffodils.

I hope this message brings you sunshine and flowers,
And brightens your day amid springtime showers;
It comes from my heart with warm hugs and smiles,
And a kiss on the cheek that reaches across the miles.

You are the sun that warms my soul, and the moon
That cools the warm air of a summer night in June;
You are the brightest star that glows late at night,
Reaching down from the heavens – my shining light.

Above all else, you are my Angel – that is crystal clear,
It's been that way for all these years, both far and near;
You have filled my life with immeasurable joy and love,
Which is why I am so thankful for you and to God above.

REBECCA AND THE HUMMINGBIRD

From an egg smaller than a jelly bean,
Was hatched this bundle of energy;
And being so tiny it can hardly be seen,
Until it hovers near a flowering tree.

Weighing less than a five cent piece,
It darted nonstop here and there;
Until it came into view of my niece,
Waiting patiently by in her chair.

Wings beating fifty times each second,
And its little heart racing at twenty;
The approaching ruby throat stunned
Rebecca with its magnificent beauty.

Slowly raising her camera she took aim,
And at precisely the right instant –
When bird and bloom were in frame,
She captured this special moment.

Hummingbirds are a beauty to behold,
With so many tiny, delicate features:
In varying shades of red, green and gold,
One of God's most precious creatures.

It's such a rare feat to get it just right,
But due to the patience of my niece,
This photo of a hummingbird in flight
Is shared, thanks to her expertise.

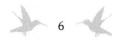

WHEN OUR EYES FIRST MET

Years after our eyes first met,
now as then it's true;
The moment I'll never forget,
falling in love with you.

It was meant to be,
we were both so sure;
Just you and me,
ideals simple and pure.

Our first kiss so tender and sweet,
it is dearly remembered;
Our first touch so soft and discreet,
to you my soul surrendered.

On the other side of the abyss
called life, I know this as such:
I'll always cherish that first kiss;
I'll never forget that first touch.

Stronger than ever before
is my love for you;
Impossible to love you more,
but that's my goal to do.

You are my heart and my soul,
my rock and my best friend;
You have made my life whole,
I will love you to eternity's end.

GOD'S COLOR PALETTE

High on the banks of a seaside rivulet,
In hues of English lavender and violet,
Stood hydrangeas, lilies and primrose,
Blushing in perfect serpentine rows.

God's color palette painted the scene,
Of heaven on earth – quiet and serene;
And gently throughout this verdant lea,
Flowers swayed at the edge of the sea.

CHANGE IS NOT EASY

Another day, and a few more boxes packed;
Before you know it, you'll be surrounded
By a maze from floor to ceiling stacked,
Leaving your family and friends astounded.

You have been magnificently energetic,
In following thru with your assignment;
Tossing the old without being apologetic,
Holding a few for your new apartment.

Change is not easy, that's for sure –
But you've been a trooper throughout;
Exhibiting the strength to endure,
And a determination never in doubt.

I marvel at your ability to begin life anew,
Without the burden of sorrow or regret;
Knowing that the remaining years are few,
Embrace the new but the past never forget.

You have my utmost admiration and respect,
For accepting your new life with aplomb;
And it's been my pleasure to help you deflect,
Chaos swirling in the midst of the storm.

But most of all, my dear, dear friend,
I love sharing these moments with you;
So, with this epistle warm hugs I send,
And a few kisses on the cheek, too!

NOTE: *The above was written for a dear and close friend, as she was cleaning out her family home of 50 years and preparing to move into a North Andover, MA independent senior lifecare facility.*

POETRY: AN EMOTIONAL JOURNEY

Writing poetry is an emotional journey consumed by *self-doubt*, expressing the writer's thoughts in prose, free verse, or rhymes *throughout*; thoughts formed by personal experiences or fantasies not lived *out*, but carried around as seeds from an active imagination to *sprout*.

The truth of the matter is that beauty is only skin deep, so they *say*; an analogy that can be applied to the meaning a poet tries to *convey* – but by writing passionately or whimsically in verse with words that *sway*, the poet's vision often runs deeper than the words on a page *display*.

The doubt lingers, to be sure, from who know *where*, that a word is missing here, or one is misplaced *there*; or that the message floats away on a wisp of *air* – adding to the poet's endless state of *despair*.

Free verse is a form of poetry that does not rhyme,
But comes together much like a conversation with self:

Is my work any good?
Why would anyone read my poetry?

Will people understand the message or deeper meaning?

Will my words be dismissed or misinterpreted in some way?
Or worse, will they generate dismissive laughter or think my work simple-minded?
Or worse yet, will they humiliate me by being critical?
Or worst of all, will they tell me it's great without really meaning it?

And even if they truly enjoy it, I will never be satisfied that it's good enough.

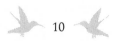

In fact, it's probably not good enough and will never be;
For a poet's work is a never-ending work-in-progress,
Fueled by insecurity and self-doubt sufficient to fill the sea,
And a genuine fear of failure impossible to repress.

Forgive me if you find this work not among the best,
As your critical eye scans the following pages;
I tried to lay it all on the line, even if I failed the test,
And will continue as the fire within me rages.

So, here I have one final thought for you to consider,
As you read each poem and deconstruct each of its verses:
Try not to be critical of the words in this poet's quiver,
For he could dip into his ink well and pull out a few curses!

SHE TOUCHED MY SOUL

Seeking a long night's rest,
In quiet, peaceful sleep she lay;
A distant moon reveals its crest
In the pre-dawn hours of a new day.

In my arms throughout the night,
Eyes never leaving her, not even to sleep;
I pray she never escapes my sight,
And leave a broken heart forever to weep.

The first soft rays of the morning sun,
Nestle in her hair and caress her face;
We refuse to rise to a new day begun,
Unwilling to end our loving embrace.

With a sigh she turns on her side,
And presses her cheek against my neck;
In waiting for her eyes to open wide,
I dare not move, not even a speck.

Sweet dreams ending...she begins to stir,
Rousing within me a million butterflies;
The fire of love that burns only for her,
Is now reflected in her wide-open eyes.

In hopeful dreams that never we part,
Are perfect memories of nights like this;
Into her ear I whisper softly to her heart,
And she touched my soul with a gentle kiss.

"Time is but the stream I go a-fishing in. I drink at it; but while I drink I see the sandy bottom and detect how shallow it is. Its thin current slides away, but eternity remains."

– Henry David Thoreau

DEAD BROOK

Below old Oak Hill's dense canopy,
It bubbles forth in protective shade,
Rising up from underground springs,
Before tumbling to a verdant glade;
Here the headwaters of Dead Brook,
Gather in a pool natural and deep,
A much remembered fishing paradise,
Where frogs croak and brookies leap.

From here the cool waters gently flow,
Between little rocks and over pebbles,
A little silver ribbon winding its way,
Into small pools as its volume trebles;
Each one creating another multiplier,
Following gravity to the valley floor,
Gaining speed all along its journey,
Perfect conditions that trout adore.

Just over the hill from my old haunts,
And moving in deep and narrow flows,
Dead Brook is protected by brambles,
Making passage akin to death throes;
But it was worth the tangled struggle,
Of fighting through there's no doubt,
For no greater thrill rewards the effort,
Than landing a hungry brook trout.

On the other side Old Man Lord ruled,
Where Dead Brook cut thru his fallow land,
Never one to cross swords with for sure,
Granting access was his line in the sand;
From here she wanders under Rt. 131,
Under a bridge and thru a meadow,
Following the edge of an old stone wall,
Into the forest where hardwoods grow.

Upon entering, the woods come alive,
The wind whispers and the world listens,
Dry, brittle leaves rustle under feet,
The filtered sun upon the water glistens;
A cacophony of familiar sounds begins,
Chipmunks chatter and songbirds sing,
Then come moments of deathly silence,
Until a spooked pheasant takes to wing.

Many days I fished this special place,
As a young boy in love with nature,
Alone with peaceful thoughts of life,
Were memories made to treasure;
Dead Brook is a part of who I am,
Measured by a narrow sliver of time,
As my young mind was free to wander,
In dreams of places pure and sublime.

HEAVEN ON EARTH

Heaven on Earth is an old fishing lodge,
Filled with rods, reels and fishhooks;
Maps, creels, and other hodgepodge –
Old friends, old scotch and old books.

MAINE TIDES

Surging forward to Maine's rugged granite coastline,
Deep tides of blue-green waters spray their briny mist,
Caressing the fragrant tips of juniper, spruce and pine,
Before retreating back again to resume the cosmic tryst.

The rhythmic ebb and flow repeats every twelve hours,
Its saline waters flooding the low-lying coastal shores,
Imposing the will of their heavenly seductive powers,
Over the livelihood of fishermen tending their oars.

The familiar routine of this daily ritual is nothing new,
It's been going on since the beginning of Mother Earth;
And will continue for as long as the moon orbits on cue,
And our planet circles the sun, well outside of its girth.

FISHIN' IN THE MIDDLE OF A STREAM

I have this recurring dream,
Of a quiet, patient old man,
Fishin' in the middle of a stream;
Alone, according to His Plan.

Cast after long, looping cast,
The delicate hand-made fly,
Settles gently upon the fast,
Cool waters rippling by.

Drifting onward to its destiny,
A swirling eddy dark and deep;
Under limbs of a broken tree,
Uprooted from the riparian heap.

A perfect place for a Mayfly,
To dance upon the flow;
While a large, sharp eye,
Looks up from deep below.

But always there is doubt,
From who knows where;
That I may hook a trout,
Yet I don't really care.

I'd rather the fish remain,
Living among its peers;
In its natural domain,
For many more years.

JOHN LARRABEE

Happy am I to live the dream,
Of a quiet, patient old man;
Fishin' in the middle of a stream,
Alone, according to His Plan.

A WORD ABOUT "MORNING GUESTS", WHICH APPEARS ON THE NEXT PAGE...

One of life's simple but cherished pleasures for me is to rise before dawn to sit in my favorite chair with a cup of coffee and a book. The chair sits next to a window overlooking the backyard.

The final verse of "Broken Dreams" by W. B. Yeats came to mind one morning while sitting 'in the one chair' waiting for the birds to join me in our shared routine of welcoming a new day.

"The last stroke of midnight dies.
All day in the one chair
From dream to dream and rhyme to rhyme I have ranged
In rambling talk with an image of air:
Vague memories, nothing but memories."

MORNING GUESTS

In the early morning hours,
Darkness is slow to retreat;
Dew lingers on the flowers,
A grassy bed at their feet.

By the window quietly I sit,
Shades open, book in hand;
Beneath the lamp brightly lit,
Waiting for their command.

Breakfast ready to be served,
To those earliest to rise;
At a pre-dawn hour reserved,
For the faithful and the wise.

A new day's light yet to appear,
But the chorus has begun;
Voices so familiar to my ear,
Cheering on the rising sun.

Over the horizon's crimson breast,
The first rays flicker at five plus ten;
Greeting my early morning guests,
The Cardinal, Bluebird and Carolina Wren.

THE COOPER'S HAWK
AND THE MOURNING DOVE

In the middle of a long walk,
On a splendid winter day;
Soared a mighty Cooper's Hawk,
Just a short distance away.

With eyes fixed on its prey,
And talons at the ready;
It proceeded without delay,
On a line true and steady.

As the mourning dove cooed,
Its final mournful tones;
The hawk claimed her food,
Devouring all but the bones.

The Long Tooth of the Hound appears on the next few pages to show the stylistic differences between: 1 – open (or free) verse; 2 – rhyme; and 3 – prose. The reader will note at once that I am not an expert on any of the three styles, but I do enjoy the challenge of making them sound pleasing to the ear.

Perhaps I could have chosen a better example than hounds on a trained hunt for those of us who are animal lovers, but it just happened that I was in an experimental mood while writing this particular poem.

THE LONG TOOTH OF THE HOUND – 1

The silver moon lay low over the tree line,
and the field where cattle grazed last summer
lay white with snow and untouched;
like a tablecloth stretching to the trees.

A sudden sense of happiness gripped me...

It was the illumination of the field;
the chill in the air,
the silence in the trees,
the darkness that was waiting.

It was the anticipation of the event...

The sound of men talking in low voices,
cigarettes hanging loosely from their lips.
High-powered search lights being tested.
Shotguns locked and loaded.

It was also the excitement of the chase...

The gathering of the dogs
straining against their owner's leashes,
baying at the scent of the night's prey
as they wait to be cut loose for the chase.

JOHN LARRABEE

And, finally, it was the success of the hunt...

The training and the preparation,
and the tracking and the pursuit
of the night's formidable prey,
until it's finally found
the long tooth of the hound.

THE LONG TOOTH OF THE HOUND - 2

A full moon was rising in the late night sky;
And where cattle grazed in last summer's breeze
A field lay white with a fresh blanket of snow –
Like a tablecloth stretching to the trees.
A sudden sense of nostalgia grips me
As memory unveils the cold wintry scene:
The illumination of the field, the chill in the air,
The surroundings so splendid and pristine.

The men gather 'round in great anticipation,
Speaking in low voices under darkened skies;
Clouds of cigarette smoke linger in the cold air
As they laugh and swap their harmless lies.
Final preparation for the hunt was underway:
Plans reviewed, double-checked and noted,
Compass readings fixed, search lights tested,
Extra ammo for shotguns locked and loaded.

The excitement of the hunt was about to begin:
With dogs tethered and led to the camp's base,
They quickly picked up a scent of the night's victim,
And were cut loose to eagerly begin the chase.
A successful hunt is dependent on many things:
Training, preparation and tracking to the sound,
For the night's formidable prey will not relent –
Until it falls under the long tooth of the hound.

THE LONG TOOTH OF THE HOUND - 3

A full moon was rising in the late night sky, and where cattle grazed in last summer's *breeze* a field lay white with a fresh blanket of snow - like a tablecloth stretching to the *trees*. A sudden sense of nostalgia grips me as memory unveils the cold wintry *scene* - the illumination of the field; the chill in the air; the surroundings so splendid and *pristine*.

The men gathered 'round in great anticipation, speaking in low voices under darkened *skies*. Clouds of cigarette smoke linger in the cold air as they laugh and swap their harmless *lies*. Final preparation for the hunt was underway: plans reviewed, double checked and *noted*, compass readings fixed, search lights tested, and extra ammo for shotguns locked and *loaded*.

The excitement of the hunt was about to begin. With the dogs tethered and led to the camp's *base*, they quickly picked up a scent of the night's prey and were cut loose to eagerly begin the *chase*. A successful hunt is dependent on many things: training, preparation and tracking to the *sound*, for the night's formidable prey will not relent - until it falls under the long tooth of the *hound*.

Some of My Favorite
Nursery Rhymes

NURSERY RHYMES

My childhood days of old,
Are remembered as simpler times;
When stories bright and bold,
Came to life in nursery rhymes.

Mary Had a Little Lamb,
Which sounds like a scam;
But there was never a merrier soul
Than that of **Old King Cole.**

Humpty Dumpty sat on a wall,
And unfortunately had a great fall;
No one could catch him from below,
Not even **Eeny, Meeny, Miny, Moe.**

Three Blind Mice
Rolled the dice;
And carelessly stole mittens
From the **Three Little Kittens.**

One, Two, Buckle My Shoe,
Said the little girl to who knows who;
I want to go outside where it isn't so noisy,
And play a game of **Ring Around the Rosie.**

Little Boy Blue tooted his horn,
To keep cattle out of the corn;
While the cat and the fiddle
Danced to **Hey, Diddle, Diddle.**

PRECIOUS WERE THE HOURS

The Farmer in the Dell
Started a family: that's swell;
But he left nothing in the cupboard,
For dear **Old Mother Hubbard**.

Peter, Peter, Pumpkin Eater,
Had a wife but couldn't keep her;
So he led her by the arm,
To where **Old MacDonald Had a Farm**.

Little Bo Peep fell fast asleep,
While tending a flock of sheep;
Because a mouse ran up the clock,
According to **Hickory Dickory Dock**.

Pat-a-Cake, Pat-a-Cake, Baker's Man,
Bake me a cake as fast as you can;
While the stove is heating a pot
For a bowl of **Peas Porridge Hot**.

A-Tisket, A-Tasket,
A green and yellow basket;
Was sitting in the corner,
Next to **Little Jack Horner**.

Rain, Rain, Go Away,
Come again another day;
But if you must stay afloat,
Row, Row, Row Your Boat.

Little Miss Muffet
Sat on her tuffet,
And right next to her,
Sat an **Itsy, Bitsy Spider**.

Rub-a-Dub-Dub,
Three men in a tub;
Which sounds wiggy,
To **This Little Piggy**.

There Was an Old Lady Who Lived in a Shoe
With so many children she knew not what to do;
One was sad and walked around with a frown,
Claiming that **London Bridge is Falling Down**.

Georgie Porgie pudding and pie,
Kissed the girls and made them cry;
But when the sun set over the hill,
Order was restored by **Jack and Jill**.

Star Light, Star Bright,
I wish I may I wish I might;
How I wonder what you are,
Twinkle, Twinkle, Little Star.

These are some of the nursery rhymes
That amused me in earlier times;
Some are timeless and still familiar today,
Those that are may surprise you anyway.

Surviving the ages as if spun from gold,
These treasures delight the young and old;
So, before the hands of time pass you by,
Read them once again to understand why.

"Sometimes I sits and thinks.
Other times I sits and drinks,
But mostly I just sits."
– **Neal Cassady**

MY RED SOLO CUP

With the lights turned down
And the music turned up,
We float 'round and 'round
Like a bug in brandy...
In my red Solo cup.

As the evening wears on
We keep the pace up,
Without so much as a yawn
Until the time comes to...
Refill my red Solo cup.

We danced the night away
Until the sun came up,
Then standing in the doorway
She waved goodbye to me...
And my red Solo cup.

JAY'S MOUNTAIN CABIN

High in the Blue Ridge Mountains of NC,
By the side of a cold mountain stream;
Tucked under a deciduous green canopy,
Sits Jay's cabin made of post and beam.

This is God's Country pure and simple,
With nary a neighbor for a country mile;
Where old Jay can holler and whistle,
Or do whatever else that suits his style.

A perfect place on the porch to relax,
And let the busy world pass him by;
Or chop some firewood with an axe,
To start building next winter's supply.

So at night when the sun goes down,
To take the chill off he builds a fire;
And like a king with a golden crown,
Sits at the throne of his private empire.

I RISE BEFORE THE DAWN

The accrued years are many,
And those remaining are few;
It needn't come as an epiphany,
That life waits not for me or you.

So however many ticks remain,
On Old Father Time's clock;
We have no right to complain,
Of the faint sounding *tick-tock*.

Scarce is a night full of sleep,
As I toss and turn in thought;
For there is much left to reap,
Before death renders it naught.

But I rise before the dawn,
And sit at my writing table;
Refusing the impulse to yawn,
Writing away while I'm able.

For I have much on my mind,
That I would like to share;
Before the neurons decline,
And I lose my way there.

So, thanks if you made it this far,
And think me not a clown;
Or as dim as the most distant star,
For what I have written down.

APPALACHIA

On a mountain top in Appalachia's Tennessee,
Beside the cool blue waters of a natural tarn,
Wildflowers grow as far as the eye can see;
From the lowland meadows to the old barn,
Where grandpa plays the harmonica for free –
And grandma knits away with a ball of yarn,
While Junior keeps time slapping his knee,
Watching the sun go down, not giving a darn.

In the front yard a family hound cocks its ear,
While chained behind the picket fence gate;
And lifts its head in a mournful song so clear,
Baying a harmonious rhythm that's first rate.
The resident barn cat looks on with a sneer,
And the cow and old nag join the chorus late;
Barnyard chickens run round and round in fear,
As a grey fox makes plans to decide their fate.

With a warm wind blowing the stars around,
And in the air apple blossoms smell so sweet;
Grandpa gathers the fiddle from the ground,
And begins a-pickin' and a-pluckin' a new beat.
A few wild turkeys are cool to the new sound,
As they swing and sway while tapping their feet;
But the wildflowers nodded off and frowned,
Having to rise early, they were all bittersweet.

From near and far gathered both kith and kin,
Singin' and square dancin' in the early night;
While Billie Bob, Bobby Jo and Rumpelstiltskin
Played their tunes under the full moon's light.
Banjo, jugs and a washboard added to the din,
Echoing thru the valley below without respite;
Slowing only after the moonshine ran thin,
And grandpa and grandma bid all a goodnight.

MORNING AND EVENING RITUALS

I sit at my writing table laboring over the words
To describe the scene outside my window;
The sun is rising – and the sound of song birds
Approaches its familiar morning crescendo.

I raise a hot cup of Joe held high with a formal nod,
As some step to the edge of the rushing waterfall;
And others are busy at the feeders atop an iron rod,
Competing to draw my rapt attention, one and all.

The scene fades into night at the close of each day,
When twilight slowly creeps behind the sleepy hill;
The moon's faint thin horn points to the Milky Way,
And daylight fades to the song of a Whippoorwill.

I bid them adieu for the evening as I tip my glass,
A few drops of Scotch over a block of ice;
Wishing them well until a new day comes to pass,
Which, as we all know, will be here in a trice.

ANTICIPATING THE FOUR SEASONS

WINTER is giving up its frigid grip at last...
>The light over the field is growing longer;
>the cold arctic air is becoming a bit milder;
>the trees are awakening from their slumber.

SPRING is coming on fast...
>The grass is turning green in the hollow;
>the tulips and daffodils are certain to follow;
>and the busy bee works like there's no tomorrow.

SUMMER promises to be a blast...
>The long warm days and short cool nights;
>the thunderstorms, rainbows and northern lights;
>the mountains, beaches and other vacation sites.

FALL will reappear just as in the past...
>The leaves of autumn will drop and scatter;
>the crows will increase their noisy chatter;
>the garden's bounty will be served on a platter.

THE SILVER BAG AND THE GOLDEN CUP*

High above the waters of Penobscot Bay,
A silver moon loomed large and bright;
And off in the distance a faint Milky Way,
Was visible on this cool summer night.

Casting my eyes to the distant horizon,
Just above the ocean's foaming sprays;
I waited for the morning's rising sun,
To caress the earth with its golden rays.

Reaching up high from the edge of a crag,
Just after the sun rose all the way up;
I gathered the moon and stars in a Silver Bag,
And placed the sun in a Golden Cup.

* W. B. Yeats made effective use of the Silver Bag and Golden Cup reference. It renders such a fairy tale image that I have used it on multiple occasions.

BROKEN DREAMS

All night long in restless slumber,
I awaken from broken dreams;
And curse the dreaded number,
That on the old clock gleams!

As the fading black ink of night,
Lingers on the window pane;
I shuffle into my study to write,
Words for a simple quatrain.

The mighty struggle has begun,
To recall the psychic scenes;
Before the earliest rays of sun,
Fix upon the window screens.

So I hover over my writing table,
To the point I want to scream;
While I ponder if life is but a fable,
A mere dream within a dream.

"You can choose your friends,
but you sho' can't choose your family;
an' they're still kin to you no matter
whether you acknowledge 'em or not
an' it makes you look right silly
when you don't."

– Harper Lee, To Kill a Mockingbird

SITTING BY THE WINDOW

A nor'easter was blowing hard outside,
With the high winds whistling nonstop,
And the old farmhouse began to shiver,
When the temperature began to drop.
Like dandruff falling from the heavens,
Came the relentless onslaught of snow,
Laying a white blanket across the fields,
And covering the trees from head to toe.

A little boy was sitting by the window,
Looking out at the snow that night,
With his sad face staring back at him,
Through the veil of a dim candle light.
His heavy breath on the windowpane,
After it was repeated once or twice,
Concealed his melancholy reflection,
Under a thin, cloudy sheet of ice.

Seeping through the cracks and gaps,
And around leaky windows and doors,
The cold air crept into the old house,
Dragging snow across the frigid floors.
As the storm intensified into the night,
And the house grew colder by the hour,
The wood stove needed a ready supply,
Of firewood for the flames to devour.

With the loss of power from the grid,
And the wood box dangerously low,
His mother and sisters huddled together,
With heavy woolen blankets in tow.
Staying warm and hoping for the best,
As the worsening situation grew dire,
The little boy trudged out to the barn,
To dismantle stalls to burn in the fire.

Weakening as night turned to dawn,
The storm left several feet of snow,
Creating a bright winter wonderland,
As the first rays of sun cast its glow.
Where the open fields stretched out,
Like a white tablecloth between trees,
The snow's thick, hard crust glistened,
In the morning chill of an arctic freeze.

After shoveling a walkway to the barn,
Then one to where the outhouse stood,
The little boy continued to tug and pull,
Dry boards from the barn for firewood.
The rays from the sun's golden arc,
Could not warm the bitter cold air,
Which held them in its vice-like grip,
Filling them with dread and despair.

Smoke drifted over the old farmhouse,
As the sun slumped lower in the sky,
And the little boy resumed his place,
Next to the window and began to cry;
Not at his face reflecting back at him,
But at the figure staggering to the door –
Fearful that a beating was forthcoming,
For his dismantling of the barn's floor.

NOTE: This poem is based on my recollection of an incident that occurred when I was 8 years old and we lived in an old farmhouse in Waldo, Maine. My father had left on an ice-fishing trip up north with a couple of his buddies. He left us without any dry firewood, which was not that unusual.

He returned the day after a bad snowstorm and I was worried that he would be upset at me for tearing down part of the barn to burn in the kitchen stove to keep us warm. The property was not ours – we were tenants.

APPLE BLOSSOMS IN HER HAIR

I walked among the sugar maples,
Shortly after crawling out of bed,
And cut and peeled a sturdy branch,
And attached a hook to a thread;
And when Mayflies were on the wing,
And distant stars were flickering out,
I dropped the hook in the eddy,
And caught a little rainbow trout.

After placing it on the ground,
With a patch of grass as its frame,
I heard a rustle in the trees,
And someone call out my name;
I turned to see a golden Angel,
With apple blossoms in her hair,
Darting in and out of the bower,
In the early morning's misty air.

She led me to an apple orchard,
Where soft rays of filtered light,
Caressed the silver and golden orbs,
Cool from the full moon's night;
She flittered from one to the next,
Touching them one by one:
Silver apples of the moon,
Golden apples of the sun.

She lifted me up and flew me back,
To the sugar maples by the stream,
Where we sat upon its grassy banks,
As I continued living my dream:
Watching Mayflies on the wing,
And distant stars flickering out,
I dropped a hook in the eddy,
And caught a little rainbow trout.

Inspired by W. B. Yeats' "The Song of Wandering Aengus"

A MAGICAL AND STARRY NIGHT

They met on an early summer evening,
At the city park by the edge of the bay;
Where lovers croon and sparrows sing,
In the hazy mist of a cool ocean spray.

There she stood, a glowing apparition,
Radiant in the soft blush of twilight;
So sweet and tender upon his vision,
Reflecting the loveliest form of light.

She beckoned with an elegant stroke,
From across the ocean-side sward;
And by her graceful movement spoke,
In the language of an ancient bard.

On Cupid's wings they swiftly flew,
Into open arms spread wide;
And from that moment they knew,
Their love was not to be denied.

In a forgotten language they talked,
Two lovers under a fading twilight;
Hand in hand they wooed and walked,
Deep into a magical and starry night.

As the silver moon slowly crossed the sky,
Its image reflecting on the dark sea below;
They embraced as the morning drew nigh,
In a moment of bliss that set them aglow.

JOHN LARRABEE

With stars sparkling in her bright eyes,
Opened wide in a warm, loving gaze;
A tender kiss prompted passions to rise,
And quickly set their hearts ablaze.

Two souls on that night became one,
Each inseparable from the other;
And they pledged under a rising sun,
A promise to never love another.

MY HAPPY PLACE

In my youth I wandered hither and yon,
To escape a life that was confusing to me;
Often starting out at the break of dawn,
Roving betwixt the mountains and the sea.

But my sanctuary - or my Happy Place,
Was in the forest under the filtered shade;
Where the scents and sounds and space,
Created a world where dreams were made.

Those lofty woods with forests wide and fair,
With their beds of moss and blankets of flora;
Wrapped me in a peaceful embrace there,
As I enjoyed its enchanting, timeless aura.

It's the place I escaped to on long summer days,
And slept under the stars on cool autumn nights;
Where I hunted and fished in its soft misty haze,
Or on a clear evening gazed at distant star lights.

It's where I listened to birds sing and frogs croak,
Where I caught a glimpse of the busy bumble bee;
And tallied the many languages the forest spoke,
Under the long branches of its variegated canopy.

This natural world helped make me self-reliant,
Teaching me lessons I still hold dear to this day;
To listen, to observe, and strive to be patient,
And to forgive and forget the pain of yesterday.

A few years ago I began writing poems on the back of our Christmas cards, which are always family photos. The next two poems were written in 2018 and 2019.

FEELING BLESSED

Not long ago we were in our prime,
When swiftly passed the hours;
How noiseless falls the foot of Time
That only treads on flowers.*

Now we're over the hill and in decline,
But happier we could never be;
Life is good and continues to shine,
Thanks to our beloved family.

The Rigsbees – Angel and John,
Love at first sight was their fate;
Then, 19 years ago arrived Payson,
 And two years later, sister Kate.

The Larrabees – Travis and Heather,
Introduced us 14 years ago to Jack;
And soon after Owen, his little brother,
Came Anna at the back of the pack.

They are our legacy to the human race,
So it's fair to say we passed the test
Of making this world a better place;
And for that we are feeling blessed.

Wishing you a Merry Christmas
and a happy, healthy and exciting New Year!

2018

* These two lines belong to William Robert Spencer (1770 – 1834)

'TIS THE SEASON

'Tis the season of reflection and celebrations,
From Thanksgiving to New Year's Eve;
Traditions passed down thru the generations,
Bookends to Christmas for those who believe.

Giving Thanks for the bountiful lives we enjoy,
And that we are so privileged to experience;
To the less fortunate we strive to bring joy,
With offerings of hope and resilience.

Arriving at an appropriate time on the calendar,
Thanksgiving serves as an important prelude
To the birth of Jesus under Bethlehem's star;
Where lying in a manger He first debuted.

The solemn remembrance of this important event
Highlights our annual season of reflection;
A prolog to honoring His 40 days of Lent,
When we briefly submit a desire for rejection.

Time stops for no one, which is hardly a mystery,
So we hope you found 2019 a year of plenty
As it fades into the expanding space of history;
And that a bright New Year awaits you in 2020.

Wishing you a Merry Christmas,
Along with a Happy and Healthy New Year!

2019

*"We don't inherit the earth
from our ancestors,
we borrow it from our children."*
– **Native American proverb**

KATAHDIN

To the west a fiery sun descends behind a hulking Katahdin,
Its distant rays yielding to the orbit of Mother Earth;
Towering oaks and gentle pines are among its worthy kin,
Surrounding the mass of silvery granite since its birth.

To the east a new moon rises above the cold North Atlantic,
Its reflection caressing the waves of an incoming tide;
Surging swells racing to the shores of Eastport are gigantic,
And crash upon the rugged coastline where they died.

The Great North Woods is reposed in soft shades of twilight,
As the Milky Way faintly appears in the early evening sky;
Wildlife begin their solemn rituals before day turns to night,
Internal clocks announcing the circadian rhythm is nigh.

A bald eagle soars high over the waters of Moosehead Lake,
Scanning the surface in search of supper for her brood;
While the shrill call of a loon awaits an answer from its mate,
And a red-tailed hawk scans the meadows for food.

Nights belong to creatures of the wild – large and small,
Some prowl restlessly for prey after leaving their beds;
Others sleep in their lodges of sticks against a muddy wall,
Protected from predators seeking their furry heads.

As the waning moon descends toward the western horizon,
To the waters of the wild Allagash it bids adieu;
And Katahdin glows like the throne of a king in the rising sun,
As God's Plan for another day begins anew.

NATURE IS ALL AROUND US

Under heaven's blue canopy,
We get to explore;
The natural world's panoply –
Who could ask for more?

The dichotomy is stark,
Between Nature and us;
The former a vast park,
The latter a muss.

Take a walk with me,
And I'll prove it true;
If you will just agree,
To give Nature its due.

Take it not for granted,
Nor ignore its space
'Round the world planted,
To protect the human race.

From the air we breathe,
To the food we eat;
From the sights we see,
To the bogs of peat.

From the sounds we hear,
To the smells we savor;
From the climate so dear,
To the water we favor.

JOHN LARRABEE

From under the surface,
Where mycorrhizae thrive;
To the edge of space,
Where astronauts survive.

Nature is all around us,
In places obvious and not;
And to us falls the onus,
To preserve the whole lot.

SUMMERTIME

Warm days
Cool nights
Misty haze
Bright lights

Golden sun
Silvery moon
Daytime fun
Evening swoon

Birds sing
Frogs croak
Bees sting
Crickets spoke

Roses bloom
Trees blossom
Clouds loom
Rains come

Tender crops
Flower beds
Dew drops
Fiddle heads

Mayflies
Hummingbirds
Brookies rise
Sacred words

NATURE'S SPLENDOR

Standing tall in the wetland marshes,
Alone and bare against the grey morning sky;
Weather-worn with stubs where branches used to grow,
A beacon for grackles and other birds on the fly.
Nature's splendor is all around us,
And changes with each blink of the eye;
With a beauty so spectacular and profound,
We look around in wonder, and sigh.

The images above are of two grackles from a series of photos taken by my niece, Rebecca Tripp. While Rebecca was shooting the photographs, her first thought was that the lower grackle was going to attack the one already perched atop the tree – and that a terrible fight would ensue. However, as the photos reveal, quite the opposite happened.

Photos: Rebecca Tripp

FOUR SEASONS

Spring is ushered in by the Vernal Equinox,
On March twenty or twenty-one each year;
It's around the time we reset our clocks,
And Old Man Winter is placed on the bier.

Spring breathes freshness and renewal,
As the sun rises a little earlier each day;
Warming the cool beds of the jonquil,
Tulips, and daffodils along the pathway.

And as skies turn to a soft azure blue,
And leaves are budding on the sassafras,
Spring hangs in the air like drops of dew,
Clinging to blades of the morning grass.

Summer Solstice appears in mid-June,
On the twentieth day in the 2020 year;
Perfect for a ride in a hot air balloon,
Or witnessing the happy bride's tear.

Summer wilts in the high, hot sunshine,
Sending crowds to the sandy beaches;
Seeking relief in the ocean's salty brine,
And from the jet stream's cool air breezes.

Soon will the dog days of August be here,
Bringing late afternoon thunderstorms;
And seasonal changes to the atmosphere,
Once again returning to the cyclical norms.

Autumn Equinox marks the start of fall,
On September twentieth or twenty-first;
Following the same quarterly protocol,
Since the beginning of time unrehearsed.

Autumn is a most splendid time of year,
With vibrant and colorful foliage galore;
A reminder that Thanksgiving is near,
And to be thankful for a world we adore.

Soon the shorter days and longer nights,
Will usher in yet another seasonal change;
When cooler air exposes crisp moonlights,
And the stars seem to be closely in range.

Winter Solstice arrives in mid-December,
The twentieth or twenty-first as usual;
Making the cycle so easy to remember,
Arriving quarterly and right on schedule.

Winter is the season of ice and snow,
Of short days and long cold nights;
And when the cold north winds blow,
And the sky is aglow in Northern Lights.

Skies seem clearer in the cold winter air,
The stars are brighter, and the moon too;
As they sparkle and it beams an icy stare,
A warning to shelter before we turn blue!

ALL OF GOD'S CREATURES ARE PRECIOUS

On a recent walk along our local golf course
I observed a giant spider web high off the ground
and connected to a pair of fairway evergreens.

Never before had I witnessed such a display:

A huge rectangular piece of art
suspended high above the ground,
with a rather large, hairy spider at its center –
waiting for a fly to unceremoniously drop by.

From my youth I learned the ways
of man's power over all other creatures.

Deer flies were to be squashed before
they escaped with a piece of exposed flesh.

Midges and mosquitoes were to be crushed
before they extracted a smidgen of precious blood.

Spiders were smashed before they could escape the boot,
and harmless snakes decapitated without a thought.

Even fireflies were sought after
for their glowing abdomens
to adorn a pinky,
or a ring finger.

Larger creatures, too, were on the receiving end
of a careless regard for life:
many died for their bounty,
others for their pelts or fly-tying plumage.

Rabbits, deer and fish for sport and food for the table.

None of this was ever done with the thought
that another form of life was being destroyed.
No, it was done simply to avoid minor discomfort
in the case of our winged antagonists;

or out of an ignorant fear of fuzzy insects
and non-lethal but slithering creatures
that raise the hair on our arms and
send shivers down our spines;

and out of the thrill of the hunt for wild game,
or the excitement of watching a brook trout
rise from the depths to swallow a well-placed fly.

This was done all in the name of
pain,
fear,
sport,
and protein for the diet.

These were the only conscious considerations
that separated life from death.

Now, as my own life nears its end I have a new-found appreciation
for all living things.

PRECIOUS WERE THE HOURS

No longer ignorant of God's creatures,
both large and small,
and more aware of the beauty of life,
regardless of the form –

I now understand the importance of brushing aside
those annoying little insects,
or giving up the thrill of the hunt,
or the excitement of the catch.

All of God's creatures are precious and deserve to live
to the fullness of life as He intended,
without cutting short the lives of the hunted
at the thoughtless whim of the hunter.

AN EAGLE SOARS

Unpacking the 4-Runner upon our arrival,
At a cottage along Swan Lake's eastern shore;
I heard what sounded like a baby chick peeping
From behind as I reached inside the back door.

And as the sound grew louder I turned to see,
A majestic bald eagle swoop down to the grass;
With wings spread wide and talons outstretched,
It plucked its prey from the riparian morass.

An unexpected and wonderful experience,
To see it gracefully soar above the lake;
And back to its brood with a reptilian treat,
Of a long, dangling and writhing snake.

I could not believe the magic of this moment,
A perfect start to our family's Maine vacation;
Where the deep, cool waters lap the shoreline,
And wildlife surrounded us in every direction.

A LOVE STORY

Time stops for no one as the years slip quietly by,
Unnoticed 'til destiny's shadow begins to appear;
Only then do we pause and reflect on the reasons why,
And lament the dizzying speed of each new year.

As life races to its rendezvous with eternity,
Think not of the path not taken, or unfulfilled goals;
But in all its splendor and boundless energy,
The joy of love and how it nourished our fragile souls.

For no greater purpose in this world can we achieve,
Than to love and be loved in all its magnificent glory;
And that with all our strength and wisdom believe,
In our own deeply intense and passionate love story.

A love story not only of earthly shapes and forms,
Answering to the intimate call of our carnal desires;
But to our emotional, intellectual and spiritual norms,
Sating the hunger of our souls before Time expires.

Living life to its fullest is the greatest love story of all,
Intoxicating the senses and fulfilling our dreams;
Leaving shadows forever etched on memory's wall,
A reminder of a world filled with heavenly scenes.

Herein lies the essence of a love story's intense beauty,
Or the art of living life without regret or fear;
Observe the awe of our natural world as a call to duty,
That nurtures our soul and renders life dear.

JOHN LARRABEE

Forsake the material nature of our inner inclinations,
And observe the natural bounties that surround us;
Only then will we fully realize the Higher Revelations
That make our life here on earth so truly wondrous.

A DREAM WITHIN A DREAM

At the end of another long day,
Side by side – hand in hand;
Talking about a better way,
Dreaming of a faraway land.

Arms wrapped around each other,
In a warm and loving embrace;
With dreams of being together,
To a bright new world they race.

Hearts merge in the moonlit night,
Whispers of promises tossed around;
Vowing never to give up the fight,
They start to drift off without a sound.

Soon forgetting the daily struggle,
With grateful hearts beating as one;
They relax into a tender snuggle,
'Til dawn welcomes the morning sun.

In quiet, peaceful sleep she lay,
Her head resting upon his chest;
Magical dreams coming her way,
As a distant moon reveals its crest.

In his arms throughout the night,
Her cares slowly drifted away;
And after the dawn's early light,
He felt her stir from where she lay.

The sun's early rays pierced the dawn,
Touching her hair and caressing her face;
Her hopeful dreams now all but gone,
But tonight new ones will take their place.

Now I leave you with this to ponder:
Is each day all that we see or seem –
Or have you ever stopped to wonder,
Are we living a dream within a dream?

"Though the road's been rocky,
it sure feels good to me."
— **Bob Marley**

I do not recall where I read the following quote, but it reminded me of the small farming community where I was born. Well, technically I was born in Belfast, which was the closest town with a hospital, but I have always considered Swanville as my birthplace.

> *"Once in his life a man ought to concentrate his mind upon the remembered earth, I believe. He ought to give himself up to a particular landscape in his experience, to look at it from as many angles as he can, to wonder about it, to dwell upon it."*
> – N. Scott Momaday

Momaday's quote prompted me to write *Swanville Is My Birthplace – Maine Is My Home*, which begins on the following page.

SWANVILLE IS MY BIRTHPLACE –
MAINE IS MY HOME

Little Swanville hamlet has been the source of many dreams,
A land of dense forests, open meadows and foaming streams;
It's the land I am proud to claim as my spiritual place of birth,
And where the tired bones of my ancestors rest in its earth.

My first unsteady steps treaded lightly upon its rocky soil,
Land tilled and nurtured by my grandfather's sweat and toil;
And in my grandma's kitchen filled with aromas so sweet,
Of assorted cookies, spice cake, apple pie and mincemeat.

My mind and body took shape among Maine's varied plats,
Where I picked crabs and dug clams from the salty flats;
And in its winding brooks and streams I fished for trout,
Casting a fly to lure the wily prey from its watery redoubt.

Long, harsh winters and cold, muddy springs were the norm,
As we hovered 'round the wood-burning stove to stay warm;
Then came the short summer months to plow verdant fields,
Of vegetables, fruits and grains did the land offer up its yields.

With summer harvest stretching into the early months of fall,
The root cellar swelled with filled canning jars lined wall-to-wall;
Along with carrots, rutabaga, turnips and honey from the bees,
Stood barrels of potatoes and apples protected from the freeze.

But, before the north winds returned and winter began anew,
Came the time to fill the larder with wild game and homebrew;
Essentials for surviving the long, harsh Maine winters of old,
When food and drink were stored to survive against the cold.

Hunting was a way of life – combining necessity and sport,
Taking wild game for their meat, for we had a family to support;
And I will never forget Maine's natural beauty and lively themes,
From the coast to the North Woods where the wildcat screams.

Times were different then, and I'm happy to have experienced it,
Invaluable life lessons that taught me to work hard and never quit;
These are a few of the experiences that shaped who I am today,
Swanville is my birthplace and Maine is my home, I'm proud to say.

Thanks to my ancestors who cleared a path for me to follow,
I had a chance to succeed without yielding to voiceless sorrow;
Fresh Maine air filled my lungs upon exiting my mother's womb,
And may my last breath exhale the same before entering the tomb.

AN EMPTY WELL

I am long past my days of youth,
But pleasant memories linger still;
Of Uncle George and Aunt Ruth,
Who gave me shelter from the chill –

And the abyss of an empty well,
Where stones stood cold and dry;
A place where fear used to dwell,
And hopes and dreams went to die.

They gave me comfort and support,
And reasons to laugh and to hope;
They were clearly the optimistic sort,
Who placed me on an upward slope –

To pursue my hopes and dreams,
With purpose and without fear;
And into the abyss came sunbeams
Of renewal that I still hold dear.

So by extending their helping hand,
My future would no longer dwell;
Or die among the stones that stand,
Cold and dry in an empty well.

REBECCA IS HER NAME

Her voice so soft and sweet,
Her smile warm and radiant;
Her mind incapable of deceit,
Her soul gentle yet resilient.

But behind that happy face,
Some dark memories reside:
A world that belies her grace,
Where old demons go to hide.

The wounds run wide and deep,
And immeasurable is the pain;
There's no escape – even in sleep,
But she copes under the strain.

Now her world is about to change,
By reclaiming control and power;
To live her life to its fullest range,
Blossoming like a spring flower.

To me she is such an inspiration,
This young lady without fame;
And it is with pride and affection,
That I say Rebecca is her name.

A GHOSTLY SHADOW

A ghostly shadow of unknown origin,
Flashes across the ceiling and walls,
Around corners and down the stairs,
A cellar-dwelling ghoul in overalls;
A vaporous form of floating ether,
Darting about before taking flight,
Challenging me to follow it down,
Down into the darkness of the night.

It can appear at virtually any hour,
Especially when it's least expected,
To frighten hosts and guests alike,
In this old house long ago erected;
This unsettling ghoulish shadow,
Has often appeared in my dreams,
And shaken me from a sound sleep,
With haunting, mournful screams.

Resolved to face this deep mystery,
One night I decided to take a stand,
And followed the haunting shadow,
With nothing but a flashlight in hand;
It glided quickly down to the cellar,
In the dreams of my drowsy slumber,
And I cautiously watched it disappear,
In the corner under scraps of lumber.

Resolute to end this enduring dream,
By not allowing the shadow to hide,
I upended the pile of lumber scraps,
And found a little old man inside;
He cowered in the corner and pleaded,
Begging me not to turn him away,
For he was just hungry and homeless,
And only needed a place to stay.

Suddenly it was no longer a mystery,
As I stared at the frail little old man,
And saw myself looking back at me,
From another life, a different plan;
I picked him up and held him tight,
This ghostly reminder of the past,
His shadow with mine is now one,
Following my every step to the last.

NOTE: *A Ghostly Shadow* is based on a periodic dream that haunted me for many years until I could stand it no longer. The dream simply would not go away until I got so fed up with it that I convinced myself that the next time the dream occurred I would follow the shadow until I found its source. I was able to do that, and I have not had the dream since!

I try not to read too much into dreams, but in this particular case (along with one other that I may tackle in verse later) I have a strong suspicion that it's unfailing consistency and frequency over a long period of time did have a deeper meaning.

I can't help but think it was connected in some way to my early childhood when I was consumed by a deep sense of hopelessness, and that the man in the dream was me as my life was then destined to unfold.

Since my life turned out much better than I could ever have imagined, I believe the dream was also a reminder that no matter how well my life turned out it could easily return to that dark state of hopelessness.

Our shadow is not just a reflection of who and where we are at any given moment in time – it also shares the burdens and joys of our past and carries the hopes and dreams of our future.

"Nothing is ours, except time...
certain moments are torn from us,
some are gently removed,
and others glide beyond our reach.
Hold every hour in your grasp.
Time is the one loan which even
a grateful recipient cannot repay."

- **Marcus Aurelius, the second century philosopher and Roman emperor who wrote the classic Meditations.**

VERTIGO

It strikes quickly and without warning,
In the afternoon, evening or morning;
And the time and place don't matter
When your world is about to shatter.

It begins with a sudden loss of equilibrium,
Followed by a confusing sense of delirium;
Then all hell breaks loose in a violent roll,
As the world starts spinning out of control.

Like a tornado's funnel touching down,
It churns the abdomen round and round;
Until the whirling dervish has emptied out,
The nauseous stomach like a water spout.

Time is of the essence to find a place,
To lie down in a quiet and safe space;
Because walking or even crawling along,
Is out of the question, even for the strong.

What dilemma could cause so much fear?
Imbalance of equilibrium in the inner ear;
An invisible yet dangerously insidious foe,
By the cosmic sounding name of Vertigo.

NOTE: About twenty-five years ago I was diagnosed by a doctor at Massachusetts Eye & Ear in Boston as having Meniere's Disease, which is an incurable and chronic hearing loss of unknown origin that is often accompanied by vertigo. My hearing loss eventually deteriorated to the point where I had to have a Cochlear Implant installed in my left ear in March 2015.

These recurring bouts of vertigo can show up at any time and usually require a minimum of 24 hours of bed rest. For a time, I kept a journal describing in detail the time of day, what I was doing at the time, and what I had eaten to see if there was a symptomatic pattern. There was none. There was no predictability to the frequency (they could occur two days in a row or two months apart), but the severity was always very intense.

Fortunately, I have not had a serious incident since 2018, which I am incredibly thankful for, but it is known to become dormant for a period of time before suddenly returning to antagonize its victim. Hopefully it will remain dormant, because I have experienced nothing that compares to the suddenness of the attacks nor the severity of the nausea that accompanies them. – JL

THE COVID-19 CORONAVIRUS WALK

On my daily walk early this morning,
My mind was more focused than usual;
Because of a national health warning,
Social distancing was the new normal.

So I thought about which was worse,
The COVID-19 coronavirus or the cure;
And if I should now reserve a hearse,
If my old worn out bones fail to endure.

My walk was an education all by itself,
A lesson on natural and human nature;
It would be hard to find on a bookshelf,
A book written of similar nomenclature.

There was a dry mist floating in the air,
Thick with fine spores of allergic pollen;
And with each breath that I could bear,
Took into my lungs a few that had fallen.

This is a natural phenomenon to be sure,
But one that can cause great distress;
Unless precautions are made to ensure,
That our lungs avoid unwanted stress.

And then there is the human side of this,
Where social distancing is taking place;
Which isn't as bad as drinking koumiss,
But might lead to saving the human race.

Except that I have to sometimes wonder,
If the cure is worse than the disease;
When people I meet hike over yonder,
Afraid if they pass me I might sneeze.

So instead of using the wide grass strip,
Between me and the divided parkway;
They hit the street with a hop and a skip,
Without a care for cars passing that way.

Therefore I have reached the conclusion,
That regardless of the rough road ahead;
To COVID-19, pollen, accident or confusion,
We must not surrender by staying in bed!

NOTE: This is a revised version of the original poem, which was written during the early stages of the COVID-19 Pandemic in March 2020 and sent with an email commenting on the virus to family and friends.

I decided to change the final stanza in the original because it sounded too macabre given the increasingly fatal nature of the virus. Here is the original final stanza for those who understand my outlook on life (and death):

Therefore I have reached the conclusion,
That regardless of the method we wed;
COVID-19, pollen, accident or confusion,
'Tis a fact that we will all soon be dead!

Burt Payson with son Dennis (1957 – 2018),
my brother-in-law and nephew.

It would be impossible to find two nicer men. Dennis loved golf so much that he bought Traditions Golf Club, turning it into one of the best golf courses in Maine before his unexpected passing in 2018.

GOLF IS NOT ALWAYS MEASURED
BY THE NUMBER OF STROKES

The sun's early morning rays seep thru the high pines,
And settle gently on the finely manicured grounds below;
It's soft glow slowly dissolves the morning's heavy dew,
As a fine, hazy mist rises above the swirling thermals.

These lush surroundings offer a temporary repose,
From the hectic lives and daily chaos of a busy world;
Leaving behind our responsibilities for a period of time,
We pursue the unreachable goal of mastering the unattainable.

Golf is a journey that can take many twists and turns,
Reaching euphoric highs and descending to exasperating lows;
A unique test of one's patience and resolve, or even one's sanity –
But in the end it's just a game, and we are blessed to be part of it.

The key to enjoying golf is not in pursuit of the unattainable art of
        perfection,
Or by becoming hostage to the numbers recorded on a scorecard;
But by the cherished companionship of friends,
And enjoying the beauty of the natural world that surrounds us.

Beyond the fairways, bunkers, and fast greens
Another world beckons with the sights and sounds of a different life;
A world many of us take for granted until ours starts to slip away,
And we suddenly realize what it means to be truly alive in this one.

PRECIOUS WERE THE HOURS

So, the next time a ball sails into the woods following an errant swing,
Or comes to rest in a watery grave just short of landing on the green;
Or burrows its way into the sand of a strategically placed bunker,
Stop, take a deep breath and gaze up at the clear blue sky.

This is why you are here in this place and at this moment in time,
Not to obsess over the unpredictable flight of a golf ball;
But rather to enjoy the pleasure of spending a few hours with friends,
And observing the sights and sounds of the natural world around us.

Like the beautifully striped chipmunks or bushy-tailed squirrels
Conspiring to interrupt the unwanted intruders in their backyard;
Their noisy chatter warns others to avoid these strange invaders
As they playfully chase each other like young mischievous children.

An unseen orchestra plays a symphony high in the treetops:
Chickadees, finches and sparrows singing their quaint repetitive songs,
While a blue jay objects with an occasional sonorous note of defiance,
Or a robin hops along the tree line gathering food for her young family.

A deer and her fawn may peacefully meander across a fairway,
Pausing to smell the air to check out the curious bystanders
Before disappearing behind the protection of the nearby forest;
A family of rabbits eats nervously under the shade of an ancient oak.

The simple movement and faint sound of leaves rustling in the trees,
A cool breeze in our faces – the sun's rays kissing the back of our necks;
Azaleas, rhododendrons and dogwoods bursting with color,
The low droning sound of a mower, and the smell of fresh cut grass.

So, let this be a reminder that the best rounds of golf
Are not always determined by the number of strokes;
But are more often measured by the quality of friendships,
And enjoying some of the natural wonders of this beautiful world.

NOTE: This is an example of "free verse" or "open verse" style of poetry. Not a very good one, but an example nevertheless. For a good example of free verse poetry, read some of Mary Oliver's works.

AFTERLIFE

Behind the silhouette of a lonely cedar
Sits a lovely honey-pale moon,
Suspended in the nighttime ether,
On a warm summer eve in June.

Dippers sparkle in the midnight sky;
A small one pours the ink of night
Into a big Drinking Gourd waiting by,
Pointing to Polaris shining bright.

And off in the distance far, far away,
Swirling 'round in the faint heavens;
My naked eye catches the Milky Way,
Alive with so many dancing maidens.

And as the limitless universe expands,
Stretching to the edges of infinity;
Beyond the inter-galactic wastelands,
Lies Aurora's soft glow of eternity.

Standing alone gazing up at the scene,
I know what God has in store for me:
An afterlife in a place not yet seen,
But one of peaceful bliss and serenity.

While writing *Afterlife*, I discovered some interesting facts about the nighttime sky. Please see my notes beginning on the next page...

NOTES:

1. I knew that the North Star held special significance as a guiding light, but I was not aware that its celestial name is "Polaris", and that it is the brightest star in the constellation of Ursa Minor.

2. I was also unaware that the Big Dipper was referred to as the "Drinking Gourd" by American slaves who tried to escape to the north. They discovered that by following an imaginary line connecting the two outer stars (bottom to top) of the Big Dipper to the star at the end of the Little Dipper's handle (the North Star) they could easily find their way north.

3. Aurora is Latin for Goddess of the Dawn.

It was quite by accident that I wrote *Afterlife* on February 26, 2020, my 73rd birthday. I do think about my age and the limited time that I have left in this world, but I do not dwell upon it.

I have always been interested by the inherent conflict between science and faith – or evolution vs. intelligent design. The science supporting evolution is very compelling, but the unfathomable size of the universe suggests to me that there is so much more that lies beyond our scientific ability to understand.

This was recently confirmed to me after reading *The Language of God: A Scientist Presents Evidence for Belief,* by Francis Collins, the leader of the international Human Genome Project that revealed the complex structure of DNA sequence – "the heredity code of life."

Near the end of the book, Dr. Collins writes:

*"Will we turn our backs on science because
it is perceived as a threat to God...?"*

and

*"Alternatively, will we turn our backs on faith, concluding that science
has rendered the spiritual life no longer necessary...?"*

His answer should comfort us all...

*"Both of these choices are profoundly dangerous. Both deny truth.
Both will diminish the nobility of humankind. Both will be devastating
to our future. And both are unnecessary. The God of the Bible is also
the God of the genome. He can be worshipped in the cathedral or in the
laboratory. His creation is majestic, awesome, intricate, and beautiful
– and it cannot be at war with itself. Only we imperfect humans can
start such battles. And only we can end them."*

FATAL ODDS

Across the millennia, human events have all
Survived the myths of gods,
Threatening lightning bolts and thunder;

Only to be swept away to ages past recall,
And fulfilling the fatal odds
Of our destiny's deep and final slumber.

IT WAS ALWAYS MEANT TO BE THUS

As our life approaches its inevitable end,
Old sorrows yield to a quiet, peaceful stage;
And our minds and body calmly descend,
Into the gentle rhythms of graceful old age.

Each new sun arrives as a welcomed gift,
Our hearts warming to its rise as before;
'Tho its daily race across the sky is swift,
We enjoy its gentle setting even more.

Lasting reflections of a long and blessed life,
Dance along the setting sun's rays;
Faded memories of real or imagined strife,
Give way to those of happier days.

No way to know when the final day arrives,
Nor is it something worth dwelling upon;
Whatever time remains in our worldly lives,
We must enjoy before the days are gone.

By savoring each minute of every hour in the day,
A living memory we make of each moment;
And God's great gift of earthly life will not betray,
Nor cause us to question His final judgment.

The swift hands of Father Time are not our friends,
But a new, infinite, unknown world awaits us;
Fear not the advancing day when our own life ends,
Rest assured, it was always meant to be thus.

NOTE: *The idea for this poem came from a touching soliloquy from "The Brothers Karamazov" by Fyodor Dostoevsky, one of the great Russian writers of the 19th century. Dostoevsky's writings were introduced to me by my son, Travis.*

A GOLDEN ANGEL

Walking along the familiar path,
Shortly after rising from my bed,
My eyes were focused on the horizon,
Where the sun would soon be red;
And when birds were on the wing,
And distant stars were fading fast,
I continued on my morning journey,
Enjoying memories from the past.

Slowly following the well-worn path,
A palette of wildflowers as its frame,
I heard a sudden rustle in the trees,
And a soft voice call out my name;
I turned to see a golden Angel,
With apple blossoms in her hair,
Darting in and out of the bower,
In the early morning's misty air.

She led me to a tree-filled orchard,
Where soft rays of filtered light,
Caressed the silver and gold orbs,
Cool from the full moon's night;
She flittered from one to the next,
And touched them one by one:
Silver apples of the moon,
Golden apples of the sun.

Then she sat upon my shoulder,
This golden Angel of heav'nly bliss;
And whispered, 'I will lead the way',
As my cheek felt her gentle kiss;
Soon she gently lifted me by the hand,
But before ascending all the way up;
She gathered the moon and stars in a Silver Bag,
And collected the sun in a Golden Cup.

Inspired by W. B. Yeats: *The Song of Wandering Aengus*

NO TIME FOR SORROW

Life is too short, so the saying goes,
Enjoy life to the fullest is the goal;
So stop and smell the blushing rose,
For it's your life and you are in control.

Father Time slows down for no one,
So live for today, plan for the morrow;
And enjoy each trip 'round the sun,
For a busy bee has no time for sorrow.

DEATH COMES TO US ALL

The majestic oak stands alone,
its leafless branches spread wide
against the nighttime sky;
a snowy field at her feet.

A full moon sits above the horizon,
its bright disk suspended
behind Her Majesty's throne;
shadows dancing on the snow.

Wispy clouds floating on high,
their faint strands of grey,
revealing the brightest of stars;
worthy jewels for her crown.

A great horned owl clutches a limb,
its keen eyes scanning
the hunting fields below;
waiting – patiently waiting.

By the edge of the snowy tree line,
in a nest of leaves visible
only to the sharp-eyed hunter,
field mice nervously slumber.

And o'er the crest of the snow-laden hill,
in the bright moonlight
of this cold December night;
two stags clash for supremacy.

Death comes to us all
according to God's will;
we can die in our sleep,
or He can spare us in battle.

NOTE TO *HER MAJESTY'S THORNY CROWN* APPEARING ON THE NEXT PAGE:

As is often the case, I will tinker with my writing (both verse and prose) incessantly. My tinkering usually results in a few minor changes to words or rhythm in verse, or to improve the flow in prose without substantially altering its overall content or meaning.

In this case, however, I took the previous poem, *Death Comes to Us All*, and re-worked the words and rhythm to give it a much different style. I'm not sure it worked as intended, since both are written in free verse, but here it is nevertheless.

HER MAJESTY'S THORNY CROWN

A majestic oak stands alone
at the crest of a barren hillock,
its gnarly feet hidden under a thick white blanket.

Its leafless branches are spread wide,
reaching for the sky as their twisted shadows
dance upon the pillows of new fallen snow.

A full moon lurks over the sleepy hill,
its bright disk providing a perfect backdrop
suspended behind Her Majesty's thorny crown.

Wispy white clouds float by in eerie silence
As a great horned owl glides into view.
It clutches a limb stretching outward –
a dark silhouette up against the full moon.

Its keen eyes scan the hunting fields below
as it sits perfectly still...
waiting – patiently waiting.

At the edge of the snowy tree line,
in a nest of leaves visible only to the sharp-eyed hunter,
field mice slumber away.

And o'er the crest of the snow-laden hill,
in the bright moonlight of this cold December night,
two stags clash for supremacy.

Death comes to us all according to God's will;
we can die in our sleep,
or He can spare us in battle –
and we get to live another day.

THE BLINK
OF AN EYE

Light reflects off objects
and is captured by our eyes,
giving us a visual sense
of our physical world.

With each blink of the eye
a new world emerges.
The old one has passed
into history's time capsule,

forever to be held by eternity's
timeless grip on the universe –
and with or without us,
the world moves on.

Steadily, inexorably, it rotates
and orbits the sun each day,
bathing us in bright sunlight
and drowning us in deep darkness

as it silently floats, unnoticed,
among a sea of shining stars.
This world belongs to nobody,
but it's ours to share for a brief moment

as we enjoy this human experience
masquerading as life:
a fragile physical state
that ends with the blink of an eye.

A JOURNEY OF THE MOST WONDERFUL KIND

Blessed are the memories of long ago,
That warm the heart with embers aglow;
For they keep the flames of hope alive,
By filling the soul with a will to survive.

Some memories of old will soon depart,
Falling tenderly, yet sadly, upon the heart;
Or dance along the sun's long mellow rays,
A gleaming reminder of our younger days.

Celebrate the youthful memories of yore,
By recalling those carefree days and more;
But don't fail to embrace the unfolding scene,
Of a long life in full bloom, quiet and serene.

A lifetime of sunshine and a few showers,
Beckons us to stop and enjoy the flowers;
Or to sleep on the crest of a clovered knoll,
Lost in dreams betwixt the stars and the soul.

It's life as a whole that we should embrace,
Not just the passing days of youthful grace;
So, with confidence and joy we should agree,
To enjoy life to the fullest and lasting degree.

And I say to those who begrudge or despair:
Live to a ripe old age with nothing to spare;
Exercising the body and focusing the mind,
Marks a journey of the most wonderful kind.

THE WANING YEARS

Behold the glorious pageant of the waning years,
With the unfolding lives of younger generations –
Full of promise as the end of my own life nears;
A reminder that life is a series of celebrations.

Sore muscles and achy joints grab me here and there,
Forceful witnesses that old age is not a state of mind,
But the start of a journey that leads me somewhere –
Somewhere beyond the world I must leave behind.

As the senses continue their slow and steady decline,
Some things just don't smell the same to my nose;
Or taste quite like a glass of my favorite red wine,
But memories will never betray the scent of a rose.

Failing eyesight and hearing are daily warnings,
That I have reached life's final winter season;
Yet I still look forward to bright sunny mornings,
Full of hope and promise for a different reason.

Although Father Time has yet to stake his claim,
The fullness of this earthly life is in plain sight:
A family for which I could not have taken higher aim,
And a few close friends to which I had no right.

Before my time runs out I bid this final farewell,
To all my loving and forgiving kith and kin –
You have fed my poor soul for such a long spell,
And made me who I am from deep within.

JOHN LARRABEE

Destiny called us together and left its indelible mark,
On so many special memories that I now hold dear;
And in another time – another place beyond the dark,
I shall be patiently awaiting your spirit to reappear.

AFTERWORD

Rare is the individual who truly enjoys reading poetry, so if you made it through to the end I am humbled – and if you found one or two poems that resonated with you, I am grateful.

I started writing poetry for fun a couple of years ago. When the number of poems reached twenty-five or so I thought of compiling them in a notebook for my children and grandchildren. Then the number grew to fifty, and I had visions of one hundred. I have still not reached the century mark, but I hope to one day.

It was never my intention to make these poems available to the public.

My joy was in the writing, not to see my name on the cover of a book – and that has not changed.

My goal was to leave something behind that my grandchildren might enjoy sharing with their children someday, not to make money – and that has not changed, either.

While reading *Precious Were The Hours*, you no doubt noticed a few photo credits and a couple of poems written for my niece, Rebecca Tripp. Rebecca had a severe spinal cord injury in 2007 that left her paralyzed from the waist down.

Prior to her injury, Rebecca was an avid outdoor adventurer, enjoying mountain climbing, hiking, biking and camping. The closer to nature she can get, the happier she is.

She has also been an animal rights advocate since childhood, even becoming a vegetarian at the age of thirteen and later a committed vegan. Following her injury, Rebecca spent much of her time as a volunteer and an active board member for Peace Ridge Sanctuary, a farm animal sanctuary located in Brooks, Maine.

I had sort of lost touch with Rebecca until I learned in March of this year that she was about to be admitted to Maine Medical Center in Portland, Maine.

She was scheduled to undergo reconstructive surgery to repair two deep pressure wounds that had become dangerously infected and threatened her pelvic bone structure. It was only then that I learned that she had been on full bed rest for the previous two years in an attempt to allow the pressure wounds to heal on their own.

The long-term success rate for this particular type of surgery is only 15%. One can understand why, knowing that *she will have to lift herself up off the wheelchair for at least one minute every fifteen minutes of every day for the rest of her life.*

All of the proceeds from the sale of *Precious Were The Hours* will be used to help fund the purchase of a standing wheelchair for Rebecca. That will allow her to perform limited activities in an upright position - and, more importantly, it will help reduce the recurrence of pressure wounds caused from sitting.

So, I am doing the unthinkable and asking you to buy more copies of *Precious Were The Hours* for your families and all your friends. They can be ordered from me or directly from Amazon. (Heck, while you're at it buy an extra one for the dog to chew on!)

Once again, thank you for reading *Precious Were The Hours* – and for being a part of Rebecca's recovery efforts as she struggles to beat the long odds of success. The hours truly are precious.

Finally, to all my friends and family – and even those previously unknown to me but who may have stumbled upon these pages, I leave you with the final two stanzas of *The Waning Years*:

Before my time runs out, I bid this final farewell,
To all my loving and forgiving kith and kin –
You have fed my poor soul for such a long spell,
And made me who I am from deep within.

Destiny called us together and left its indelible mark,
On so many special memories that I now hold dear;
And in another time – another place beyond the dark,
I shall be patiently awaiting your spirit to reappear.

John Larrabee
2020

Additional copies of *Precious Were The Hours* may be purchased directly through **Amazon.com**, or by contacting the author at:

Email: **preciouswerethehours@gmail.com**
Mobile: 978-360-1901

NOTES

NOTES

NOTES

_____

_____

_____

_____

_____

_____

_____

_____

_____

_____

_____

_____

_____

_____

NOTES

_____

_____

_____

_____

_____

_____

_____

_____

_____

_____

_____

_____

_____

NOTES

NOTES

Made in the USA
Middletown, DE
06 September 2020

18200543R00078